The Real Story of Puss in Boots

David Foxton

A SAMUEL FRENCH ACTING EDITION

SAMUELFRENCH-LONDON.CO.UK
SAMUELFRENCH.COM

Copyright © 1997 by David Foxton
All Rights Reserved

THE REAL STORY OF PUSS IN BOOTS is fully protected under the copyright laws of the British Commonwealth, including Canada, the United States of America, and all other countries of the Copyright Union. All rights, including professional and amateur stage productions, recitation, lecturing, public reading, motion picture, radio broadcasting, television and the rights of translation into foreign languages are strictly reserved.

ISBN 978-0-573-06497-5

www.samuelfrench-london.co.uk

www.samuelfrench.com

For Amateur Production Enquiries

United Kingdom and World excluding North America

plays@SamuelFrench-London.co.uk

020 7255 4302/01

Each title is subject to availability from Samuel French,

depending upon country of performance.

CAUTION: Professional and amateur producers are hereby warned that *THE REAL STORY OF PUSS IN BOOTS* is subject to a licensing fee. Publication of this play does not imply availability for performance. Both amateurs and professionals considering a production are strongly advised to apply to the appropriate agent before starting rehearsals, advertising, or booking a theatre. A licensing fee must be paid whether the title is presented for charity or gain and whether or not admission is charged.

The professional rights in this play are controlled by Samuel French Ltd, 52 Fitzroy Street, London, W1T 5JR.

No one shall make any changes in this title for the purpose of production. No part of this book may be reproduced, stored in a retrieval system, or transmitted in any form, by any means, now known or yet to be invented, including mechanical, electronic, photocopying, recording, videotaping, or otherwise, without the prior written permission of the publisher. No one shall upload this title, or part of this title, to any social media websites.

The right of David Foxton to be identified as author of this work has been asserted by him in accordance with Section 77 of the Copyright, Designs and Patents Act 1988

THE REAL STORY OF PUSS IN BOOTS

First presented at Dewsbury Arts Centre by the Dewsbury Arts Group on 27th November 1995, with the following cast:

Martha Winterhedge	Elma Dowson
Puss	Jemma Hopkinson
Colin Miller	Simon Fletcher
Caleb Miller	Stuart Marshall
Cinderella	Jessica Hyde
Drusilla	Janet Ullyott
Blusilla	Gloria Appleton
The King	Gary Clayton
Lord Dandini	Chris Perkin
Ogre	Francesca Burns

Directed by David Foxton
Designed by David Foxton
Lighting by Andy Wright

CHARACTERS

Martha Winterhedge, an Irish Fairy Grandmother
Puss, a cat (referred to as him but could be a her)
Colin Miller, a poor man: our hero
Caleb Miller, Colin's cruel stepbrother
Cinderella, the poor girl next door
Drusilla, a stepsister to Cinderella
Blusilla, another stepsister to Cinderella
The King, a king
Lord Dandini, a chancellor
Ogre, an ogre

SYNOPSIS OF SCENES

ACT I
SCENE 1   Outside two poor houses
SCENE 2   Inside the same houses

ACT II
SCENE 1   The King's castle
SCENE 2   The houses again
SCENE 3   In the forest

ACT III
SCENE 1   At the Ogre's
SCENE 2   Back at the houses
SCENE 3   The King's birthday ball
SCENE 4   House to house
SCENE 5   At the castle once again

PRODUCTION NOTE

The play was first staged at Dewsbury Arts Centre by Dewsbury Arts Group, where the stage has entrance doors through the proscenium arch L and R, which open onto an apron stage running the full width of the theatre. These entrance doors were used as the doors to the two houses and thus were visible throughout the play: the main curtain was used when scene changes had to be made. Lighting can emphasize scenes that focus on the doors while the main stage is also in use. At the beginning of the play the "pile of old clothes, rags, bags, rubbish, et cetera," was set up in front of the main curtain, allowing Martha Winterhedge and Puss to crawl under the curtain and establish themselves under the pile immediately prior to the commencement of the play. Any movement of the pile that occurs as they make their entrance only increases the audience's attention. The "pile" is cleared by Puss as instructed by Martha, being pushed under the main curtain and cleared by A.S.M.s prior to the main curtain being opened. If entrance doors are not available to be used as "house doors" then it perhaps would be necessary to create them just inside the proscenium arch, with a false "main curtain" to their rear across the stage to effect the scene changes as indicated in the script. However, individual directors and designers may devise other ways of achieving the desired results.

David Foxton

ACT I

Scene 1

Outside two poor houses

A pile of old clothes, rags, bags, rubbish etc. is in front of the CURTAIN *at the beginning of the play, beneath which are Puss and his (her) real owner Martha Winterhedge (a fairy godmother by profession). Though at most times Martha appears to be a sort of amiable "bag-lady", she can also appear in a wide variety of guises (or disguises). There are fitful movements from the on-stage heap, a few grunts (or are they snores?) occasionally. The aim should be for the incoming audience to become aware of the heap and wonder what "thing" might be under it*

The House Lights dim to black-out, leaving the pre-set only on the heap. It moves, it snores — and then suddenly erupts as Martha sits up, and stretches

Martha Aaaah! Ooooh! Begorrah! Sunday! Sunday! Isn't it? Is it? Or isn't it? Or is it Saturday? Bejabus and bally bubbles, I can't be knowing. How long have I slept? P'raps it's Tuesday — no, Thursday; that's it, it could well be Thursday, 'cos I am meself, I could murder a cup of tea   ... or is it Christmas, or Easter, or washing-day? Let me think now — what day is it really, I wonder? Yesterday was   ... what   ... no   ... today is   ... What is today?

Hopefully she will receive some response from the audience she can build on

What? Is it? Are you sure? Monday! (*The actual day*) Of course it is — wasn't I going to say that meself? Monday! I can tell, I can feel it in my bones; to be sure it's Monday, what else could it be, 'cos it's all Monday-ish, isn't it? It looks like a Monday, it feels like a Monday, it tastes like a Monday and by golly it even smells like a Monday. Just smell it, just be after taking a wee sniff; one, two, three — sniff ... There. Isn't that just about as Monday-like as you can get? Oh my word, it's certainly Monday right enough or my name isn't Martha Winterhedge — and it is 'cos I've got me initials on me bag. Will you be taking a look? See, "M.W.", that's me — and it doesn't matter which way you have it up it's always "M.W." Isn't that magic? No, course it isn't! I'm not here on my own you know — I'm not, I've got a friend, I'll show you. Come on "Puss", will you be after waking up you lazy little *spalpeen*.

Martha grabs Puss's tail and pulls him into view. He has a bag with him

Wake up you sleepyhead, you; there's things to do, stories to make up. Come along now, will you wake up? It's — it's — would you know it, I've gone and forgotten already what day it is.

She might be prompted

Oh yes, it's Monday!

Puss stretches

My word and aren't you the tired cat? You spend so long out at nights that you wear yourself out; you want to come home at a reasonable time ...

Puss sees the audience and "hides"

Now what's the trouble? What is the matter? Are you pretending to be shy and all? Look, we're all friends here; come on out and wave a paw.

Puss, hidden, shakes his head

Come along now, we've got lots to do — will you come along, be told. Here puss, puss, puss ...

Puss emerges somewhat shyly and waves to the audience

That's better. Now that didn't hurt, did it? No, of course it didn't. Now say "hallo".

Puss looks aghast and mimes "What me?"

Yes, you. Say "hallo" to the people.

Puss shakes his head and hides again

Oh dear, poor old Puss — not really shy, just takes a while to get used to situations. New situations that is. Once the talking starts he can talk the hind legs off a donkey. Once we start a story he's away like a little leprechaun and you can't be after keeping him quiet. You see, Puss and me, we're storytellers, aren't we Puss?

A nod from Puss

Act I, Scene 1

We make stories up and we make them happen, don't we Puss?

Another nod from Puss

We do it all the time. What was that one we did last week? This old memory of mine is a dreadful thing, I tell you. Remind me Puss, what was it?

A shrug from Puss

Last week's story, remember — you were in it.

Puss shakes his head

Oh yes you were. Honestly you're getting to be as bad as I am. Think, what was it now? Say something. You wouldn't think that he's the only cat that's kissed the Blarney Stone, would you? You were in that tale, I tell you, the one about that apprentice lad who became the Mayor of somewhere big ... You were his cat. What was it now? Bill ... Bill ... Worthington and his ... no ... Tom, Tom Millington and his ...

Hopefully the audience will suggest "Dick Whittington"

That's it! I'm glad you came. That's it. Dick Whittington.

Puss nudges Martha

Oh yes and his cat — that was one of ours.

If no-one in the audience assists Martha, then Puss must attempt to convey "Whittington" through mime; three syllables, last syllable "ton" = heavy weight, pound, stone, kilo, ton ... first two syllables sounds like sitting, knitting, etc.

You see, we travel around helping stories to happen, Puss and me — we do. I'm a sort of fairy godmother, and Puss is a sort of — cat, but special, clever, eh Puss? You'll see what I mean. Now then, Puss, what story is it today?

Puss pulls out a diary or similar book from his bag

Show me ... Oh yes, oh ballybananas, oh my word yes; oh you'll be after liking this one — I hope. There's a bit for you (*she gives a page from the book to Puss*) and a bit for *me* (*she takes a page herself*) and no doubt we'll meet up in the middle and see each other at the end. Now that's about as clear as mud, but you'll follow it, don't worry. Quick, Puss you clear up all our bits and pieces, ready for the start of it all.

Puss tidies up during the following, pushing everything under the curtain

I'll tell the nice people what we're at. I'm so glad you came — I am, 'cos we've got a story to do, and if you weren't here nobody would see it, and it would get written down in books later and they wouldn't get it right. You see if you're not there when the story happens, then people can tell you anything, can't they, and they do. Well, just watch this and listen because this is the real story of what actually happens ... So ... it's ... Once upon a time — we always start like that then everyone knows it's the beginning — there was a poor man who lived next door to a poor girl.

During the following Martha and Puss move off into the audience, but continue the story

SCENE 2

Inside the same houses

The CURTAIN *rises and the Lights come up to disclose two kitchens in two houses. Each house has a front door, facing the audience; through these, characters can either leave the stage or turn and enter the kitchen. The space in front of these is deemed to be "outside" the houses. Colin is seated dolefully in his kitchen and Cinderella equally dolefully in hers. A pair of boots and a polishing cloth are prominent in Colin's kitchen*

Martha The man's stepbrother was quite rich but gave no money to his younger brother, Colin. The girl's sisters were quite rich but gave no money to their stepsister, Cinderella. Now perhaps you've heard of her before, she's been in and around stories for quite some time. Come along, Puss — we'll leave 'em to it for a while. I could still be doing with a cup of tea ...

Martha and Puss exit from the auditorium

Caleb (*off*) Colin, where the devil are you?

Colin looks up

Drusilla (*off*) Cinders, are you there?

Cinderella looks up

Act I, Scene 2

Caleb (*off*) Skulking in the kitchen?
Blusilla (*off*) Come and do my hair!
Caleb (*off*) Bring my boots this minute.
Drusilla (*off*) Breakfast, quick — for two!
Caleb (*off*) Cleaned and polished, mind you!
Blusilla (*off*) Toast and tea will do — and fruit juice ——
Drusilla (*off*) — and bacon and eggs ——
Blusilla (*off*) — and fried bread.
Drusilla (*to Blusilla; off*) What about your spots, dear?
Blusilla (*off*) ... and tomatoes.
Drusilla (*off*) Ooh yes!
Caleb
Drusilla } (*together; off*) Did you hear me?
Blusilla

Colin and Cinderella nod

Caleb
Drusilla } (*together; off*) Well?
Blusilla
Colin
Cinderella } (*together*) Coming!
Cinderella Toast? Tea? Fruit juice ... Oh dear, we don't have anything at all, what am I going to do?
Colin Polish! Boot polish? Where is it? There isn't any — I used it all up. What am I going to do?
Caleb (*off*) Best boots!
Drusilla
Blusilla } (*together, off*) Breakfast!
Colin
Cinderella } (*together*) Borrow some!

Colin puts a scarf on and Cinderella puts on a shawl. They both leave their kitchens and appear through their respective front doors. They walk across the stage looking anxiously behind themselves and bump, back to back

Colin
Cinderella } (*together, ad-lib*) Oops, sorry! Pardon me! Sorry about that! Are you all right? Yes thank you. Don't worry, I'm all right ... Sorry! Thank you.

They cross to each other's door and knock. Pause

Cinderella There's no-one in, I've just come from there.

They knock again

Colin I've just come from there, there's no-one in.

They realize their situation and come together C

Cinderella Could I borrow some bread?
Colin Have you got any boot polish you could lend me?
Cinderella You see I've got to make breakfast for my two stepsisters or there's going to be trouble.
Colin And I've got to polish my stepbrother's best boots or there'll be an explosion.
Cinderella And some tea — and sugar.
Colin Black (*or brown*) it needs to be.

They shake their heads together

Cinderella What am I to do? My stepsisters will be so angry when there's no breakfast.
Colin Not half as angry as my stepbrother when his boots haven't been cleaned.
Cinderella I mean it isn't as though they haven't got any money: it's just that they never give me any to buy things with ...
Colin Same here.
Cinderella Then they wonder why we don't have any food in the house.
Colin Or boot polish.
Cinderella You can't eat boot polish.
Colin You can't polish boots with bread.
Caleb (*off*) Are my boots ready yet? Colin! Did you hear me?
Colin Oh heavens, did you hear that?
Cinderella Your stepbrother?
Colin That's him.
Cinderella Wanting his boots.
Caleb (*off*) Boots! Now!

Colin nods

Drusilla (*off*) Cinderella!
Blusilla (*off*) Breakfast!
Drusilla ⎱ (*together, off*) Now!
Blusilla ⎰
Colin And that's your stepsisters, wanting their ——
Cinderella Breakfasts! Oh dear!

Act I, Scene 2

Caleb (*off*) Are you there?
Colin Boots! Oh dear!

Colin and Cinderella sit disconsolately C on the edge of the stage. The action continues inside the house

Caleb appears in his kitchen

Caleb Do you ever pay attention to me, you wart? When I say "boots" I mean boots, and I want them now ... Colin! Colin! Where the devil are you, you worm? Have you done the boots? (*He rummages about*)

Drusilla and Blusilla appear in their kitchen, speaking as they enter

Drusilla ... and don't make my egg too runny, you know I like them crunchy hard.
Blusilla ... and I don't want soggy fried bread, you know it does nothing for my complexion.
Drusilla Cinderella!
Blusilla Where is the girl?
Drusilla ⎱ (*together, shouting*) Cinderella!
Blusilla ⎰
Caleb (*shouting*) Colin, where are you?
Drusilla Ooh, aren't they noisy next door.
Blusilla Terribly. Awfully common people.
Drusilla (*calling out to the wall between them*) ... keep the noise down, we can't hear ourselves shout.
Caleb (*loudly*) Boots! Where's my boots? Dammit!
Blusilla (*calling out to the wall between the two houses*) Don't you use language like that in the house next door to us.
Caleb Where is he? What's he doing?
Drusilla I can't imagine where she is, or what she's up to.
Caleb — and where are my boots anyway?
Blusilla I shall faint from hunger in a moment.
Drusilla No dear, I was going to do that.
Blusilla Just watch me.
Drusilla Don't you dare faint before I do; if you do I'll never forgive you.
Blusilla If you've got to go, you've got to go ——
Drusilla Hold back — show some restraint, woman ——
Blusilla I'm going ... (*She wavers*)
Caleb (*loudly*) Where are you, you toad?
Blusilla (*shouting back*) I'm in here, fainting and don't you "toad" me.
Drusilla Who does he think he is? I've a good mind to give him a piece of it.

Blusilla Of what dear?
Drusilla My mind — give him a piece of my mind.
Blusilla You could give him some of mine as well.
Drusilla Are you sure you can spare it?
Blusilla I've got plenty.
Drusilla Come on, then, let's do it!
Blusilla Right!

The sisters move out of the kitchen and emerge at their front door, just as Caleb does the same at his side

Caleb
Drusilla } (*together*) There you are!
Blusilla
Caleb (*to Colin*) Didn't you hear me shouting, eh? Didn't you?
Drusilla I should say we did. What a noise. You ought to be ashamed ...
Caleb Are the boots ready? Have you polished them?
Blusilla Who do you think we are — boots indeed!
Drusilla Don't you dare take that tone with us.
Caleb I'm not talking to you two ——
Blusilla Why? Have we upset you?
Drusilla What have we done?
Caleb (*to Colin*) Boots! Boots!

Caleb drags Colin to his feet. Colin proffers the boots and Caleb knocks them from his hand

   They're not clean, they're not polished; can't you do anything right?
Colin There's no polish!
Caleb There's always some excuse — no polish! Pah! There's no elbow grease. Don't you ever do any work?
Drusilla We know just what you mean.
Blusilla She's just the same.
Drusilla Cinderella!
Blusilla Where's our breakfasts?
Cinderella There's no bread for toast, no tea for tea, no eggs for eggs ... (*etc.*)
Drusilla See what we mean.
Blusilla Hopeless!
Drusilla Hopeless!
Caleb Hopeless!
Drusilla I shall faint from hunger.
Blusilla No dear, I was going to do that. It was my idea, remember.
Drusilla I can faint, too.

Blusilla But not like me dear, not like me ... I can feel myself going — look, watch, I'm off ... (*She wobbles*)
Caleb Oh, stop that you two.
Blusilla I beg your very pardon.
Caleb I said stop it, I can't do with you two moaning and whining — what about my boots?
Drusilla Your boots are nothing to do with us.
Blusilla Can't blame us.
Caleb (*pointing to Cinderella*) Who's that then?
Drusilla Cinderella.
Blusilla Our stepsister.
Caleb (*threatening the sisters*) Right! And when my lazy stepbrother should have been polishing my boots where was he?
Blusilla I'm going again, Drusilla, I'm away. (*She wobbles*)
Drusilla No, you can't, it's my turn ... I'm beginning to drift.

They wobble in unison

Caleb He was out here with your sister, wasting time.
Cinderella That's not true. He came to ask to borrow some polish and I was asking to borrow some bread.
Colin That's how it was, Caleb.
Drusilla
Blusilla } (*together, wobbling*) Here we go... Watch us go... Here we go...

The sisters collapse; one is caught by Colin and one by Cinderella

Martha enters through the audience ringing a small bell

Martha Hold it there! Stop! Stop!

The action on stage freezes

Don't they argue a lot? Look, look, I'm a postman now. I've got some letters to deliver, and I think I've got some for some of *you*. (*She hands out some envelopes with Christmas cards in them to members of the audience*) One for you, and you — I think. They might be Christmas cards — and I've got some for this lot, too. (*Meaning the cast on stage*) I don't think they're cards though — this one for Colin and his brother looks all official-like. It's from a lawyer, Fleecem, Grabbit and Scarper. This one for Cinderella and her sisters has got a royal crest on the back — it could be an invitation from the King to something or other. I'd better deliver them. (*She rings the bell. Shouting*) Post! Post!

Colin drops the sister he's supporting and Cinderella hers

Now let me see ... (*to Colin*) there's one for *you (she hands Colin an envelope)* and then (*to Cinderella*) there's one for you. (*She hands Cinderella an envelope*)

Drusilla and Blusilla clamber to their feet. Cinderella and Colin open their envelopes during the following. There is a letter in Colin's envelope and three invitations in Cinderella's

(*To Caleb*) You ought not to be running about without boots on, you could catch a chill.
Caleb (*viciously*) Mind your own business. Get off before I set the dog on you.
Martha (*heading for the exit*) Why is it that they always threaten postmen with dogs? I mean I quite like dogs, really ...
Caleb Did you hear me?
Martha I'm going, bally bedsteads, I'm going!

Martha exits

Drusilla Oh, I went then, dear ...
Blusilla I was away too ...
Drusilla You mean we've both been?
Blusilla I was all wafty.
Drusilla I think I was even waftier.
Blusilla You couldn't have been.
Caleb I wish you two would stop it!
Cinderella (*referring to the envelope*) Marvellous! Wonderful! At last!
Drusilla What is it?
Blusilla Should you be reading that, Cinderella?
Colin (*referring to his letter*) Oh no! Oh dear! Oh Lord!
Caleb What is it? What's the letter about? Show me.

Caleb snatches the letter from Colin and reads it

Cinderella It's from the castle, from the King: they're invitations.
Blusilla }
Drusilla } (*together*) Invitations?
Cinderella To a ball — for the King's birthday.
Blusilla Show me. (*She grabs an invitation*)
Drusilla No, show me. (*She grabs the other invitation*)

Act I, Scene 2

Drusilla and Blusilla read the invitations

Caleb Yes! Yes! I've been waiting for this ... You know what it is, don't you?
Colin I can read.
Caleb It's the result of father's will — at last!
Colin I know.
Caleb (*reading*) Dear Sirs, This is to inform you ... rhubarb, rhubarb, rhubarb ——
Drusilla A ball!
Blusilla At the castle.
Cinderella The presence is requested of ——
Caleb — the entire estate, land, houses and fortune to his son — Caleb!
Drusilla Drusilla.
Blusilla Blusilla.
Cinderella Priscilla.
Caleb It's all mine. (*He reads more*)
Cinderella — at the Grand Ball in celebration of the King's ——
Drusilla Wait a minute.
Blusilla Stop! Hold it right there!
Cinderella What is it?
Drusilla You can't go. (*She takes Cinderella's invitation and tears it in half*)
Blusilla You're not Priscilla. (*She takes the invitation and tears it again*)
Drusilla You're plain Cinderella.
Cinderella That's what you call me ... I'm really Priscilla.
Drusilla Pooh!
Blusilla Pah!
Drusilla Hoo!
Blusilla Hah!
Cinderella But ——
Blusilla No buts.
Drusilla No ifs.
Caleb (*reading*) ... and to my stepson, Colin ... (*To Colin*) Good grief, there is something for you, you wart!
Colin (*he knows*) There is.
Caleb (*laughing*) His cat — he's left you his cat! What a joke! What a laugh! You can't even feed yourself and now you've got a cat!
Drusilla (*to Cinderella*) So, no birthday ball for you.
Blusilla Just for us.
Caleb Oh, that's the best laugh I've had for years. Wait till I tell them in the village — and listen, (*he grabs Colin*) just make sure my best boots are clean when I get back, or there really will be trouble.

Caleb goes into the house and exits

The sisters head through their front door

Drusilla We'd better go and see what we can wear. Oh I'm so excited.
Blusilla So am I! So am I!
Drusilla I thought you felt weak and feeble.
Blusilla No dear, that was you. I'm quite robust.
Drusilla Oh yes, I can see that, now you mention it.
Blusilla What!
Drusilla Come on ...
Blusilla What about breakfast?
Drusilla No time for that — think of our waistlines.
Blusilla Ooh yes.

The sisters ad-lib their way off, leaving Colin and Cinderella

Cinderella Oh, that's marvellous that is, great, simply great; my big chance torn to pieces. An invitation to the ball — gone!
Colin At least you've got somewhere to live. Now I'll be turned out of the house, nowhere to go, and no money.
Cinderella Do I look like a millionairess? If I could have just gone to the King's castle: one chance, a dance with a prince and anything might have happened.
Colin Some hopes.
Cinderella What d'you mean by that? Stranger things have happened, if you're in the right place at the right time.
Colin Along comes a prince ...
Cinderella Well, it's more likely to happen at the King's birthday ball than it is here.
Colin Perhaps ...
Cinderella It is ... Of course I'd need a ball gown and jewellery ...
Colin You'd need a fairy godmother.
Cinderella That's the first thing you've said that makes sense. But where would you get a fairy godmother?
Colin At this time of night?
Cinderella What?
Colin Nothing.

Martha enters through the audience. She is still dressed as the postman and is ringing a bell

Martha Post! Post! Second delivery. (*To members of the audience, handing out envelopes*) Look here's one for you and one for you and you ... Special delivery for Colin Miller, special delivery for Colin Miller ...

Act I, Scene 2

Colin Here, that's me ...
Martha Special delivery, sign here. (*She holds out a slip or pad for Colin to sign, with a pen*)

Colin signs the slip

Cinderella Anything for me?
Martha No, sorry. You expecting anything?
Cinderella Just hoping.
Colin There we are.
Martha And there you are. (*She hands Colin a small parcel*)
Colin What is it?
Martha Special delivery. Open it and see.

Drusilla enters through the front door

Drusilla Cinderella! Inside this minute.
Cinderella Coming!
Drusilla There's a few alterations need doing to Blusilla's ball gown.

Blusilla enters through the front door

Blusilla Cinderella! You're needed to let out Drusilla's ball gown.
Drusilla Yours you mean.
Blusilla You mean yours.
Drusilla }
Blusilla } (*together*) Ours!
Drusilla Come on girl — now!

The sisters go

Cinderella Very well — bye!
Colin See you again.
Cinderella Best of luck with the cat.
Colin What? Oh yes. Best of luck with the ——
Cinderella Bye!

Cinderella exits into her house

Martha What? Best of luck with what?
Colin Just something she needs.
Martha What? What is it?
Colin Wishful thinking. I'd better open my special delivery.

Martha Never mind that: what does she need?
Colin A fairy godmother.
Martha Really?
Colin They're as rare as princes round here.

Colin exits into his house

Martha Says who? Little do you know. Rare. Bally broomsticks, I'll just be after showing him who's rare and who isn't. (*She knocks at Cinderella's door*)
Drusilla (*off*) Go away!

Martha knocks again

Blusilla (*off*) Who is it? Go away!

Martha knocks again

Drusilla opens the front door and looks out

Drusilla We're far too busy for anything. Now go away, right away or we'll set the dogs on you — and we mean it.
Martha All right! Have it your way. But I'll be back, you mark my words! I'll be back.
Drusilla Course you will — you're the postman.

Drusilla goes in and shuts the door

Colin enters his kitchen and begins polishing the boots

Martha (*heading for the auditorium exit, speaking as she goes*) You see the problem is that fairy godmothers can't actually involve themselves until they are wished for. We've got to have a sort of invitation.

Caleb enters his kitchen wearing his old boots

Caleb And I want them sparkingly clean. D'you hear me? When I come back — sparkingly clean. And then you can start packing 'cos you'll be out on your ear. (*He leaves the kitchen, speaking as he goes*) And don't be wasting any more time with that girl next door —— (*he comes out of his house via the front door*)

Blusilla appears in the doorway to her house

—— she's just as poor as you are.
Blusilla Who was it? What did you want?

Act I, Scene 2

Caleb So make a good job of it.
Blusilla Was it you?
Caleb Are you talking to me?
Blusilla Have you been knocking at my door?
Caleb Why would I want to do that?

Drusilla comes out of the house

Drusilla Blusilla! Blusilla! Where are you, we need to check the size of your gussets!
Blusilla I'm a size ten.
Drusilla Aren't we all, dear? But you need letting out.
Blusilla You must forgive my sister, young man, she's not in complete control of her faculties ...
Drusilla At least my faculties fit me.
Caleb You must excuse me, ladies.
Blusilla Ooh, "ladies" — he said "ladies".
Caleb I've got some urgent discussions to make about my inheritance.
Drusilla Inheritance?
Caleb Until later perhaps ...

Caleb exits through the audience

Drusilla He's quite a nice man really.
Blusilla Not noisy at all.
Drusilla With an inheritance; I think I like him.
Blusilla I found him first.
Drusilla Men with inheritances are hard to find.
Blusilla He's mine.
Drusilla I always thought you wanted a prince.
Blusilla No, that's what you said.

Cinderella appears in the doorway

Cinderella Who's wearing the pink?
Drusilla } *(together)* Me!
Blusilla

The sisters go into the house during the following

Drusilla Pink to make the boys wink, that's what they say.
Blusilla If they see you in pink, dear, they'll close both their eyes.

They ad-lib further as they exit. Cinderella follows them off

Colin It's going to take a while to get these boots clean. But if I do, then perhaps when Caleb returns he'll let me stay here; it's only a little cottage, and now he's got more houses, and land, and money, and all I've got is a cat and a special delivery. (*He picks up the parcel*) Well, this is a bit small for a cat. I wonder ... (*He opens the parcel. There is a whistle inside*) It's a whistle. (*He blows the whistle; it is silent*) Nothing, no sound — what a stupid idea. A whistle that doesn't. It's just another disappointment. (*He tries it again*) Nothing. (*He goes back to polishing the boots*)

Puss enters through the auditorium, addressing members of the audience during the next speech

Puss Where is it? Who's got it? Is it you? Have you got it? You? Who then? Somebody's got the cat whistle. Didn't you hear it? Is it you? Are you sure it's not you? Turn your pockets out ... No ... No ... It's not you. Who's got the silent cat whistle then? I can hear it every time it's blown, can't you? (*He blows the whistle again*) Oh! There it goes. Who did that? Was it someone over here? Is it you? Is it? Really loud it was. It goes through you ... Whoever's got the whistle gets the cat — that's me. Who's got it?

Perhaps the audience will inform Puss that Colin has it

Who? The person who lives here? Are you certain? (*If Puss has to make the discovery; indicating Cinderella's house*) It could be someone who lives here. (*He listens at the door*) No. Or could it be (*he moves to the other door*) ... here?

Colin blows the whistle

Yes! Oh yes! Ow! Ow! Ow! This must be the place! (*He knocks on the door to Colin's house*)

Colin (*surprised*) Oh no! He's not back already I hope. (*He polishes the boots a little more*) Oh, I hope not!

Puss knocks again

I'm on my way ... (*He opens the door*) Caleb! I didn't expect you back so ...

Puss bows and poses dramatically, and hands over a card

What's all this? (*He reads*)

Act I, Scene 2

> "Now's the time for Christmas cheer,
> And welcome to a good New Year,
> Share the joy and all be merry,
> With mistletoe and holly berry
> And presents too beneath the tree,
> There's some for you and some for me.
> This card a present does include,
> A free drink in the interlude."

Puss realizes it's the wrong card, and exchanges it for the correct one

Wrong card, eh? What's this then? (*He reads*) "To whom it may concern: This is your inheritance. Fleecem, Grabbit and Scarper, Solicitors." I think I'd rather have the other card. Ah well, I'd better make the best of it; after all it's not your fault, Puss, is it, eh? You can't help being my inheritance, can you? Come on, come inside ...

Colin goes into the house

Puss Well, it's good of you to take it that way, I appreciate it. I don't ask much, just food and drink, of course, and a comfortable bed — with the odd mouse thrown in for good measure.

Colin quickly returns

Colin Who said that? Who's there? I could have sworn I heard someone out here.

Colin goes back into the house

Puss I didn't see anyone (*to the audience*) — did you? There wasn't anyone else about, was there? No, of course there wasn't ...

Colin comes back again, even more quickly

Colin I heard it again. There is someone about. I distinctly heard someone talking — out here.
Puss Out here?
Colin That's right, clear as clear ...
Puss Well, I certainly didn't see anybody at all, not a soul. But I don't mind helping you look around. I'll look over here (*he points*) ... and you look over there. (*He moves to the area he indicated*)

Colin stands open-mouthed

    Nope! No-one here. I think you must be mistaken, sir.
Colin (*aghast*) It's — you ——
Puss Sorry? What's me?
Colin You spoke.
Puss D'you know, I believe I did.
Colin A talking cat. An actual talking cat.
Puss You almost got it in one.
Colin You can really talk?
Puss Yes indeed — you could well discover, sir, if I may make so bold, that your inheritance — that is me — is not such a bad bargain at all. Together we can perhaps make things happen, make situations change; who knows, just around the corner fame and fortune could be beckoning.
Colin (*still amazed*) A talking cat!
Puss (*to the audience*) I don't believe he's heard a word I said. (*He grabs Colin*) Now just listen hard: I'm a cat, and I can talk; have you received that one?

Colin nods

    Now all we've got to do is make things happen to your advantage ... Are you still receiving me loud and clear?

Colin nods

    So ... when do we start, O Master? (*To the audience*) I learnt the "O Master" from a genie I once knew.
Colin And you're going to help me?
Puss Now you're talking, or rather I am; and I'm going to help you, and we start right now ... (*He heads into the house*) Come on inside — Master.

Puss goes into the house, heading for the kitchen

Colin (*to the audience*) Wow! A talking cat — what about that?

Colin follows Puss into the house through the front door and they both move into the kitchen

Puss (*sitting*) All I need to begin to make you rich and famous is ——
Colin Rich and famous — me?
Puss Isn't that what you'd like?
Colin Yes, but ...

Act I, Scene 2   19

Puss Well then ... All I need first of all is a bag, as might be this one (*he picks one up*) and a pair of — boots, as might be these. (*He picks up Caleb's boots*)
Colin These boots — oh no. (*He takes the boots from Puss*)
Puss No?
Colin They're Caleb's boots; my stepbrother's boots: if they're not here when he comes home, then I'll be in serious trouble.
Puss But, Master: no boots, no fame; no boots, no fortune ...

Colin thinks briefly

Colin Take them. (*He passes the boots to Puss*)
Puss (*putting on the boots*) You'll not regret this, O Master, for now behold — or *voilà* as we say in La Fontaine — Puss ... in ... Boots. Now there's a title for a story if ever I heard one.

Caleb enters the auditorium

Caleb Are my boots ready yet? Did you hear me, you wart? I said "Boots"! "Sparkling" I said! I hope you haven't been wasting time.
Colin Oh heavens — he's back! Quick, give me the boots.
Puss What?
Colin The boots — I need the boots.
Puss But they're mine — you just gave me them.

Caleb bangs on the door to his house

Caleb Come on, let me in, you worm.
Colin He'll go mad! He'll go berserk! What can I do? Give me the boots back.
Puss I thought you wanted to be rich and famous.
Colin I do — but I also want to be alive to enjoy it.
Caleb (*banging more*) Did you hear me?

Blusilla emerges from her front door

Blusilla I think half the town must have heard you. Please be quiet, my sister's just having her seams let out and it's a ticklish business.
Puss Trust me, Master. Have faith ... and we can ... How big is he?
Colin Big enough.
Puss Is there a back door?

Colin shakes his head

Caleb (*banging more*) I won't tell you again. Open up.

Drusilla emerges from her front door

Drusilla Did you tell him, Blusilla?
Blusilla I did, dear, I explained about your predicament, but he wouldn't listen ...
Drusilla I say, you there; could we have a word?
Caleb You mean me? (*He moves to the sisters*) Have you a problem of some kind?
Blusilla Ooh, he's so powerful, isn't he Droo?
Drusilla He is! He is! Really overpowering, Bloo.
Colin You'd better make a run for it.

Puss nods

Caleb I don't mean to upset you ladies, but I'm just about to explode with rage and in all probability separate my insect of a stepbrother from his breath and it might be messy.
Drusilla All by yourself?
Blusilla With your bare hands?
Caleb Any minute now.
Drusilla Ooh, I feel all faint ...
Blusilla No you can't, it's my turn.

A slight argument ensues

Puss and Colin appear at their door

Colin (*stage whisper*) Quick, go now, while he's not looking.
Puss (*stage whisper*) I will; give me the bag.
Colin (*stage whisper*) I haven't got it. I'll get it.

Colin goes into the house

Puss (*shouting*) I think I left it near the stool.

There is a slight pause, almost a freeze. Caleb turns and sees Puss in his boots

Caleb (*irate*) My boots!
Puss Aaah!
Caleb It's a Puss in my boots! I'll swing for him. (*He charges after Puss*)

Act I, Scene 2

A chase through the audience follows. Puss leaps into the audience and is followed by Caleb shouting for the return of his boots. They go up one aisle and then cross the audience to the other, returning to the stage

Puss pushes Drusilla, who falls into Blusilla's arms: as she recovers her position, Caleb does the same

Colin emerges from the house with the bag (a sack), which Puss snatches as he crosses the stage. Caleb and Colin wrestle for space

Get out of my way you worm!

Puss hides in the audience. Caleb asks the audience for assistance in finding Puss: Drusilla and Blusilla start giving helpful directions and Colin tries to quieten them. Puss is then spotted by Caleb, but they are at different sides of the audience. They jockey for position. Blusilla approaches Puss from the stage, unbeknown to Puss, who does not spot her

Puss exits through the auditorium, followed by Blusilla; Caleb exits at the other side

Caleb and Blusilla almost immediately re-enter on opposite sides, somehow having missed Puss in the middle; they search for him, ad-libbing dialogue: "Where is he?" etc.

Puss appears on stage behind Drusilla, and joins in shouting instructions to Caleb and Blusilla

Then Puss is spotted. Caleb and Blusilla approach the stage warily. Drusilla grabs Puss; Colin pulls her off him

Cinderella emerges from her house with garments

Cinderella Are you going to let me try these on you?

Caleb comes onto the stage and pushes Cinderella aside. She drops the garments

Caleb Out of my way.

Cinderella falls and is suitably angry. Puss wrestles with Drusilla. Blusilla comes onto the stage and Colin wrestles with her. Caleb grabs Puss from behind. Cinderella comes up behind Caleb and kicks him hard in the rear. Caleb releases Puss, and turns: Puss bends down behind Caleb, and Cinderella pushes Caleb over him. Drusilla helps to pick him up. Puss and Cinderella shake hands

Puss escapes through the auditorium

Caleb Now where's he gone? (*To Cinderella*) You stupid girl; that confounded cat has run off with my boots.
Blusilla Leave me alone, young man, get your hands off me, you don't know where I've been.
Caleb (*to Colin*) I blame you, you toad.
Blusilla Me?
Caleb No — him!
Drusilla And I blame you, Cinderella!
Blusilla And look what she's done with our ball gowns.
Caleb So you can get out — now!
Colin Where?
Caleb Anywhere away from here; go on — out — leave — this very minute. Leave everything, just go.
Colin Go?
Caleb Go and join your precious cat!
Drusilla Cinderella! Now all this will need washing too.
Blusilla You are a clumsy selfish girl.
Drusilla Go and see to it immediately.
Blusilla Go!
Caleb (*to Colin*) Go!
Drusilla Go!

Martha enters through the auditorium

Martha Stop! Stop! Stop!

Everyone on stage pauses

(*Moving to the stage: she speaks to the audience as she does so*) It's me again. I'll just sort out their problems.
Caleb Go away — we don't need a postman!
Drusilla Come on Blusilla, we need to start getting ready.
Blusilla For the ball, of course.
Caleb (*to Colin*) And don't let me catch you round here any more.
Martha Could I have a word?
Caleb
Drusilla } (*together*) No!
Blusilla

Caleb, Drusilla and Blusilla exit through their respective front doors. Colin exits too, through the audience. Only Cinderella and Martha remain

Act I, Scene 2   23

Martha I just wanted a word, that's all.
Cinderella I really am fed up with all this. Why doesn't something go right for a change?
Martha Like what, my dear?
Cinderella Oh I don't know , it's just — that — well, I just wish ...
Martha Yes? Yes? Yes?

Drusilla emerges from her house; she drags Cinderella in during the following

Drusilla Come on, you idle good-for-nothing ... this won't get us ready for the ball.

Drusilla and Cinderella exit

Martha But, wait a minute, this could be the start of something ... Could I — I could — I can — I said ... can I ...? (*She knocks on the door*)
Drusilla (*off*) Go away!
Martha (*turning to the audience*) Oh, bally bunions!

There is a flash

  Martha disappears

CURTAIN

ACT II

Scene 1

An ante-room in the castle. The interiors of the two houses have been struck and replaced with the ante-room setting, but the front doors are still in place either side

The Curtain *rises*

There is a flash

Martha appears, now dressed as a cook

Martha Bally bodkins! I'm sorry about that, I just had to go and lie down a minute. Did you find something to do with yourselves while I was away? That's good. Look, can you tell, I'm not a postman any more, I'm a cook. I'm the cook to the King. You see the King's after holding a birthday celebration, a ball — that's like a big dance — because it's his birthday, did you know? (*If the audience respond*) Oh you did ... And so he's called in some outside caterers, people to make the food — and it's me. It's easy when you're a fairy godmother; just a wave of me magic rolling pin, and there's a banquet before you can say "Bally breadbuns!" What happened was I was minding me own business when the King said ——

The King enters with Dandini, his chancellor

King (*as he enters*) ... I wish we had someone who could cook!
Martha Just like that.
Dandini But we don't, sire, we don't.
King Are you sure? Who boiled my egg this morning?
Dandini You had toast, Your Majesty.
King Did I? Did I indeed. Who did that then, eh?
Dandini The Court Toastmaster, Your Highness.
King There we are then!
Martha He really does need some help.
Dandini You can't serve toast at a birthday ball.
King Of course you can't, whose stupid idea was that?
Martha Can I help, Your Majesty?
King Was it you? Don't deny it!

Act II, Scene 1

Martha I'm the cook you just wished for.
King Did I? What do I want a cook for, Lord Dandini?
Dandini For the ball.
King Ball? What do I want a ball cooking for?
Dandini Because we have no-one else to do it.
King (*bewildered*) Pardon?
Martha Could it be, sire, that you're celebrating somebody's birthday? And you're throwing a ball.
King I thought we were cooking it?
Dandini Allow me, Your Highness. Yes, indeed there is to be a ball, and it is to celebrate an important birthday.
Martha I thought as much.
King Fine! Fine! I enjoy birthdays. Whose is it?
Dandini It's yours, Your Highness.
King Mine? All mine? A birthday for me — again! Didn't I have one only last year?
Dandini You have them every year, Your Majesty.
King Of course I do ... We'll have a ball! That's what. And everyone will be there. I'll make an invitation list straight away; write this down.
Dandini It's already been done, sire.
King Good! Good! And the princess, my daughter, must be there; make a note of that.
Dandini Impossible, Your Majesty.
King Impossible? I demand it! And I am the King, aren't I?
Martha You are indeed, sire, you are indeed.
King So you just go and tell her she will be there — and I'm not taking "no" for an answer. Do it — this moment.
Dandini But sire ——
King Well?
Dandini I must remind you that — with respect — you haven't a daughter; there is no princess.
King Where's she gone then?
Dandini You never had one, sire.
King D'you know I could have sworn that I did. Anyway, in that case, don't invite her. If she can't be bothered to exist, then I shan't waste my time inviting her.
Dandini (*resignedly*) Sire.
King Invite the prince instead. Yes, invite my son, the prince. Or is he away ... hunting, or whatever.
Dandini No sire, he's not away.
King That's excellent then.
Dandini But — Your Highness ——
Martha (*to the audience*) You can guess what's coming, can't you?

King A problem?
Dandini I regret to inform you, Your Majesty, but you have no son.
King (*over-the-top*) No son! What news! Bereft. To have no daughter is bad enough, but then to learn about one's only son. It's too devastating, I'm truly distraught — such news at a time like this ... Will I ever recover? The shock. (*He staggers a little.*) Tell me, I can take it: how did it ... happen? Speak?
Dandini You've never had a son, sire. No daughter, no son.
King Does my wife know?
Dandini You have no wife, Your Highness.
King Do you know, I thought it was quiet at breakfast times.
Martha But, if I may make so bold, your worthiness, there could still be princes at your birthday ball, and, who knows, even the odd princess or two.
King Do you think so? Oh I do so hope you're right — whoever you are.
Martha Sure and bally baskets and aren't I after being the cook you need to make your party go with a real swing.
King Did you boil my egg this morning?
Martha Now how could it be me, when it was toast you had?
King Right — that's right. You must be my cook. Dandini — here's the cook — for the — that —
Dandini Ball.
King What? Oh yes! Yes, for the ball, the birthday ball — it all comes back to me now.
Martha So what would Your Honour be wanting in the way of good things to eat?
King What have we got?

Puss interrupts, making a splendid entrance, albeit somewhat hurriedly

Puss Your Majesty! (*He gives a flourish and a bow*)
King That's me! Isn't it?
Puss I bring greetings, and a gift from my master.
King A gift? Greetings?
Puss To you, Your Highness.
King Is it someone's birthday?
Puss (*after a pause*) Er ... well ...

Martha nods to Puss

Indeed so, your eminence.

Martha points to the King

It is for your birthday.

Act II, Scene 1   27

King Mine? Oh heavens ... I'm touched, I really am touched, aren't I, Dandini?
Dandini You are indeed, sire.
King And what is the gift you've brought me, and from whom?
Puss This very morning, Your Highness, my master, the prince ——
King The prince?
Puss Indeed so. The prince gave me this bag and commanded me to put inside it a gift fit for a King, and to deliver it to you.
King I like him enormously already.
Puss Oh you would and you will, sire, for he is the most charming of fellows.
King A prince? Charming? Well it certainly sounds right.
Dandini So what's in the bag?
Puss I'm coming to that. So I took the bag, and collecting a lettuce and a juicy carrot I went out and used them to catch you a nice tender, succulent — rabbit. (*He proffers the bag*)
King A bunny rabbit!
Puss Indeed so, Your Highness, from my master the prince.
King Now, what do you make of that, Dandini?
Dandini Pie?

Dandini takes the bag, and hands it to Martha

King What did you say?
Dandini Or casserole perhaps. Why not see what your cook thinks?
King (*aghast*) My little bunny rabbit! My birthday bunny?
Puss *Bon appetit!*
Martha I'm away to peel the onions!
King Wait! Stop! How dare you all! What awful things to say. My birthday gift from — from a prince. It's not for eating, it's a pet. Isn't that so?

Puss shrugs

Dandini If you say so, My Lord.
King For which I am most grateful. You must thank your master, the prince — charming! And he will be a guest at my ball.
Puss He will be honoured.
King Now the plans, Dandini, remind me of the plans — what are they?
Dandini Sire! Invitations are out all across the country, all the people who are anybody are agog with anticipation and exultation at the prospect of the King's birthday ball.
King Tell me more.
Dandini Sire, you can envisage the scenes ...

Everyone turns to look towards Cinderella's front door

The two stepsisters emerge from Cinderella's house (to shake and fold a table-cloth perhaps)

Drusilla Not long now, Blusilla.
Blusilla Ooh! I can hardly wait — I'm all agog you know, and exultified!
Drusilla Oooh! I'm more "gog" than you are, dear — I mean this ball could be my first chance to catch a husband.
Blusilla It could be your only chance.
Drusilla I just need Mr Right to be there.
Blusilla Well I'm looking for Prince Right, I don't want a "mister" — I mean they're ten a penny, aren't they?
Drusilla Well, I haven't noticed that myself.
Blusilla Well, I mean, take Mr-Next-Door.
Drusilla No you take him, he's too rough for me.
Blusilla He may be rough, but he's powerful, and he's strong, and he's forceful, and ...
Drusilla Ooh, don't! Don't! You'll make me "go" again.
Blusilla It's still not your turn; I've got a "go" in hand.
Drusilla I cannot help it, Bloo; when it comes over me, I've just got to succumb.
Blusilla Control yourself, you can't go about the place succumbing all the time!
Caleb (*off*) Just you wait! Just you wait!
Drusilla } (*together*) Oooh! It's him ...
Blusilla }
Drusilla It's got me legs, Bloo ...
Blusilla And mine ...
Drusilla } (*together*) And off we jolly well go ... aaaaah!
Blusilla }

They faint right away

Everyone turns to look towards Caleb's front door

Caleb emerges from his door

Caleb (*throwing a small pile of objects on the ground*) You worm! Wait 'til I get my hands on you again! You and that flea-infested moggy — in my boots, my boots. Well you're not coming back in here; your bits and pieces can wait out here for you — it's all rubbish anyway!

Caleb goes back into his house

Act II, Scene 1   29

King No, it's no good, I can't envisage anything. I can't even imagine what's happening. Let's go play with the bunny rabbit, Dandini. (*To Puss*) And don't you forget to send your master, the prince, to the ball — he might like to meet my daughter.
Dandini No, no, no, Your Highness.
King What? Oh yes — don't tell him that because I haven't got one.
Puss Very well, Your Majesty.
King Oh, incidentally, where does this prince — charming though he is — where does he live?
Puss Live? Ah yes, where indeed. He lives — he lives in the palace deep in the forest, the one with the golden spires.
King What?
Dandini What?
Martha What?
Puss It's quite high up the mountains.
Dandini But I thought the ogre lived there.
Martha The fearsome, magic, ogre lives there.
King Don't I live there?
Dandini No, My Lord, the ogre does.
Puss Ogre? Did you say ogre? Oh my!
King Well, well, it's a small world. Now it's your prince's palace. You must tell me some time how he got rid of the ogre. Come along, Dandini, make a noise like a carrot.

The King and Dandini exit

Martha Do you know, I sometimes think you take stories a bit far. Ogre indeed — and how the bally buckets are you going to get rid of him?
Puss All is possible for a ... (*With a flourish*) Puss in Boots.
Martha Well, I can't but help think that you're becoming a little too big for your boots; ogres are not so easily got rid of, you know.
Puss I'll think of something, won't I?
Martha And where's your master anyway?
Puss I'm not sure.
Martha And does he look like a prince? Has he got the clothes for it?
Puss Well, no ... not yet. Don't worry.
Martha Why should I worry, all is possible for a ...
Puss Don't say it!

Puss and Martha sit, thinking morosely

Colin enters down an aisle through the auditorium, ending up outside his front door

Colin Puss! Here puss-puss-puss! Puss in Boots, where are you? Puss!

Ideally the audience realize that Colin actually can't see Puss, for they are in two different scenes!

Oh dear, nothing's going right for me. I've been chasing after that Puss in Boots for ages: somebody even said he'd gone up to the castle to see the King — and that's miles away! (*He sees the objects thrown out by Caleb*) What's all this? My things — Caleb's thrown my things out. Now I really know that I've nowhere to live — and no money. What am I going to do? If I could just find Puss and persuade him to give the boots back ... but — wait a minute — the whistle. I could use the silent whistle. I wonder if it's here with my things? Let me see ... (*He searches amongst the objects and finds the whistle*) Yes! Yes! Look it's here. I blow it and Puss comes to me — easy! Why didn't I think of that before? Silly me.

Caleb comes out of the door behind him

All I've got to do is give it a blow ... (*He puts the whistle to his lips*)
Caleb (*grabbing the whistle*) What's this then? How long have you had this? Whose is it?
Colin Give it back, Caleb, it's mine.
Caleb I've never seen you with this before. What d'you want a whistle for anyway?
Colin I'm learning to play it.
Caleb Don't talk such rubbish, anybody can blow a whistle. You don't need to learn — watch me.
Colin No! No, don't blow it — I mean please don't blow it.
Caleb Why not? Why shouldn't I? You can't tell me what to do and what not to do — I'll blow it if I like ... (*He makes to do just that*)
Colin (*grabbing at the whistle*) No! No! *Don't!*
Caleb Don't you shout at me, you worm. I'll blow it just as much as I like.
Colin No, Caleb, don't, don't; you'll ... I mean, you can't, you mustn't, you really shouldn't.
Caleb No-one orders me about; least of all someone like you.
Colin Look! Oh, look — over there it's Cinderella's sisters, asleep; if you blow the whistle you'll waken them up.
Caleb (*with a laugh*) So I will. What a good idea — it'll give them the fright of their lives. What a good idea.
Colin Please don't do it! Please ...
Caleb (*moving to the recumbent sisters*) I'm going to enjoy this. (*He takes big breath and blows the whistle, which makes no sound*)
Puss Aargh! Don't do that!
Martha What? What?

Act II, Scene 1   31

Puss The cat whistle.
Caleb (*frustratedly*) What's the matter with it? Is it broken?
Colin What? Oh yes, yes, it's broken. It's a broken whistle.
Caleb Typical of your rubbish. I'll give it another go. (*He blows the whistle again*)
Puss Ow! Stop it! Don't do it any more. I'm on my way. I'm on my way!
Martha Where are you going?
Puss Whoever's got the whistle gets the cat — you remember!
Caleb I'll give it one more chance. (*He blows again*)
Puss (*with his paws to his ears*) I'm coming, I'm coming — just don't blow it again.

Puss exits from the castle

The CURTAIN *falls, covering the ante-room setting*

SCENE 2

The houses again

Caleb It's useless, this is — it's just like you. Useless! Useless!

Drusilla and Blusilla stir

Drusilla Did somebody call?
Blusilla Coming! Coming!
Colin Give me it back then ... if it's useless.
Caleb Why, what good is it to you?
Drusilla Ooh look Bloo, he's here — the man.
Blusilla So it is — the man ——
Caleb (*grabbing Colin; threateningly*) Come on, worm, tell me: if it's useless, why do you want it?!
Blusilla Isn't he — so — masterful?
Drusilla Isn't he — so — dynamic?
Blusilla Ooh! I could eat him.
Drusilla Ooh! I want a bite! I want a bite!
Caleb *Well?* Look, I'll blow it again; I'll show you what a waste of time it is, just like you! (*He puts the whistle to his lips*)
Colin (*grabbing at Caleb*) No!
Blusilla } (*together; also grabbing at Caleb*) Hallo, big boy!
Drusilla

Caleb swallows the whistle with a gulp. There is a pause

Colin What is it?
Blusilla What's happened?

Drusilla Are you all right?

Caleb mimes his problem

Drusilla What's the matter?
Blusilla I think he swallowed something.
Colin Oh no! Oh don't say that!
Drusilla Can he speak?
Blusilla Pat him on the back.
Drusilla You do it.
Blusilla We'll both do it.

The sisters pat Caleb on the back

Puss (*off*) Don't do that! I'm being as quick as I can!
Drusilla Nothing.
Blusilla It's really stuck.
Colin Hit him again, harder!

Caleb shakes his head, but they hit him again

Puss (*off*) Will you stop that?! I'm on my way I tell you.
Colin Turn him upside down.
Drusilla } (*together*) Ooooh!
Blusilla }
Colin Come on, grab his legs, don't just stand there.
Drusilla Come on, Bloo, grab a leg — it might be your only chance.
Blusilla What d'you mean? I've had my hands on a leg before.
Drusilla That was mutton dear, it's not the same. Come on, grab!

Colin and the sisters up-end Caleb

Colin Now shake him! Shake hard!

They shake Caleb; seemingly the whistle is dislodged. Colin picks it up

Got it! It's here! You can stop now! I've got it. You can let go.
Drusilla But I was just beginning to enjoy it.
Blusilla It's quite thrilling really — shall we give him another shake?

The sisters shake Caleb again. As they do so, Colin retrieves his things and makes a big thing of wiping the whistle etc.

Act II, Scene 1

Colin I'll leave him in your fair hands, ladies.
Blusilla We'll look after him.
Drusilla I'll pander to his every whim.
Blusilla Oh, I wanted to do the pandering.
Drusilla We'll both do it. Don't worry about him.
Colin I won't! *(He heads for the exit)* I most certainly won't ...

Colin exits

Blusilla We could take him inside and put him — to bed.
Drusilla Ooh — yes.
Blusilla Would you like that, Mr-Next-Door?

But Caleb cannot speak; he mimes as much

Drusilla He can't speak, poor fella ...
Blusilla That means he can't say "no".
Drusilla I get like that sometimes.
Blusilla So let's get him inside.

The sisters help Caleb towards the exit. He tries protesting, but to no avail

Drusilla *(as they go)* He's what they call muscular, isn't he Bloo?
Blusilla He's got muscles in places that I've only got elastic.
Drusilla We'll have difficulty getting him to bed.
Blusilla So what's new dear — we'll just have to try.
Drusilla Come on, lift your side ...
Blusilla Which way — up or down?
Drusilla Come on!

The sisters and Caleb exit through the sisters' front door. As they go, Puss runs in through the auditorium

Puss *(breathlessly)* Don't blow it again! Don't you dare! I've been as quick as I could. Just don't blow that blooming whistle any more, it's so shrill, it's vicious ... so don't ... where is he anyway? Hallo! No-one about. Well someone blew it from here — that's a fact.

Perhaps the audience will tell him what happened

I wonder where my master is. Wait 'til I tell him that he's a "prince" — or at least the King thinks he is! What I've got to do now is get him some suitable clothes for a prince and a palace. Now, listen, I need some help:

if the King, or anybody comes along and asks who this place belongs to will you tell them: "the prince"? If they ask who pays your wages, say: "the prince". Let's just try it. Pretend I'm the King.

A routine: Puss asks the audience questions and hopefully receives answers — "The prince!" — or even "The prince, Your Majesty", etc.

Great! That's fine! You can all help make my plans work. Now I'd better catch up with my master — the prince! We'll be back soon. (*He heads for the exit*) Don't go away.

Puss exits through the auditorium. As he does so, Cinderella enters through her door

Cinderella (*irate*) Another mouth to feed! I've got enough to do. I've just about finished all the work on their ballgowns, then there was breakfast, and now there's a visitor to be looked after, and the floors to scrub and polish, and the windows to clean, and the garden needs weeding, and then I'll have to start making more meals ... Oh it really isn't fair. I wish — aw, what's the point, it's no good complaining — and yet I wish ... No, that's not going to help any ... What did Colin say? "You need a fairy godmother." He was right; I wish I had one right now.

There are a flash and a bang and Martha appears

(*Taken aback*) Who are you?
Martha Now isn't that after being a silly question if you just think about it for a bit — I mean have you not just wished, and given me the invitation so to speak.
Cinderella Where did you come from?
Martha And there's another question before I've fully answered the first one. So which do you want me to answer: "Who am I?" or "Where did I come from?"
Cinderella Yes! Yes!
Martha Bally beefburgers but it's taking me all me time to be understanding you. Can you not tell who I am? I'm your fairy godmother.
Cinderella (*amazed*) You are!
Martha (*to the audience*) I always like this part — the amazement bit.
Cinderella My fairy godmother. You're my fairy godmother?
Martha (*to audience*) I think she recognizes me now.
Cinderella Wow!

Pause

Martha Forgive me for interrupting the quiet like this, but, as your Fairy Godmother, is there anything I could perhaps do for you?
Cinderella Do for me?
Martha Well, you know, wishes and the like.
Cinderella Oh — wishes. Oh yes! Oh I wish, I wish I could go to the ball.
Martha (*to the audience*) This is more like it! (*To Cinderella*) And your wish is granted; you will go to the ball, Cinderella — (*to the audience*) and you can quote me on that!
Cinderella But I've nothing to wear.
Martha Now what do you think we can do about that?
Cinderella (*after a slight pause*) Oh, I wish I had a beautiful ballgown.
Martha (*to audience*) She's catching on quick! You shall have a beautiful ballgown, Cinderella!
Cinderella And I wish I had some elegant glass slippers, and jewellery too, diamonds and pearls, and a crystal coach to ride in and footmen and a velvet cloak, dark blue like midnight sky, and an ostrich feather fan, and I wish all the floors were swept and scrubbed and the windows clean and sparkling and the meals all ready and the beds all made and ——
Martha Whoa there! Will you just hold back a wee minute, I'm trying to get these wishes sorted out in my mind. Do you think we could perhaps nip in the house and sit down with a pot of tea and make ourselves a list?

Martha and Cinderella move into the house during the following speech

Cinderella ... and the bedrooms redecorated, and all the garden weeded and a new cooker, 'cos the old one is absolutely useless, and a holiday and a fondue set and a cuddly toy ...

They are gone

Scene 3

The Curtain *between the houses rises on a forest with a palace in the distance*

Puss and Colin enter through the audience and head for the stage during the following

Puss This way, Master — just come this way ...
Colin But I don't understand, Puss, why does the King believe I am a prince ... I mean I don't look like a prince.
Puss Leave it all to me, Master; and look there in the distance, can you see it? It's your palace deep in the forest.

Colin Where?
Puss There! (*He points*)
Colin But that's the ogre's palace — everyone knows that.
Puss Not any longer; it is yours.
Colin You're joking.
Puss Trust me, Master, and it will all be yours.
Colin When?
Puss Just do everything I tell you to do ... and you will be a prince and that palace will be yours.
Colin A palace?
Puss That's right!
Colin And a prince!
Puss Correct!
Colin Charming.
Puss That's the one.
Colin So what must I do?

By now they are on the stage

Puss Take all your clothes off.
Colin What?
Puss Take all your clothes off.
Colin That's what I thought you said.
Puss Well, do it.
Colin But ... I mean ... Why? What?
Puss Trust me, Master, I want you to take all your clothes off and go and have a swim in the pool over there (*He points off*) Leave your clothes with me. Just a pleasant relaxing swim.

Colin looks unsure

Fame and fortune, Master ...
Colin Right! Right! A swim it is ...

Colin starts divesting himself of his clothes and gradually moves off throwing the items of clothing to Puss

Puss (*receiving the items; ad-lib.*) Thank you — got it, thanks, that's it. Thank you, Master, and in you go; it's not as cold as all that. It'll be very nice once you're in! (*To the audience*) Now I'll hide all his clothes, throw them away. It's all part of my plan.

Puss exits in the opposite direction to that taken by Colin

Act II, Scene 2   37

Colin (*off*) Ooh! That's cold. Ooh! Oh! Oh! Aah! That's not too bad.

The King and Dandini enter through the auditorium

King It's too bad! It's too bad of you, Lord Dandini. I mean you had it in your hands.
Dandini I know, My Lord, but it jumped, and ——
King I've never had a bunny rabbit before, and now he's gone, run off.
Dandini He bit my finger, sire, I couldn't help let him go.
King He could be anywhere, he could be absolutely anywhere, and he was my first ...
Dandini Rabbit?
King Present, Dandini, present! Because you know whose birthday it is, don't you?
Dandini Yours, My Lord.
King Is it? Well then it's even more important that we find him. Make a noise like a lettuce, Dandini, and look for him. (*He points*) You look over there.

They look along both aisles, if there are two, or take a side each, ad-libbing "Have you seen a little rabbit?" etc

Dandini It's no use, My Lord, there's no sign of him.
King Gone! Gone! Quite gone! My own little pet bunny rabbit.
Dandini Perhaps you'll get another one.
King Do you think so?
Dandini From the prince?
King Charming.
Dandini That's him.
King Dandini — who does all this place belong to?
Dandini I'll ask ...

They ask the audience, ad-libbing "Who does this place belong to?", "And who do you work for?", "Whose are these seats?" etc., etc. Hopefully, the replies they receive confirm the owner as "The prince", even "Prince Charming" or "Prince Charming, Your Highness"

King Good heavens, Dandini, I didn't realize how important this Prince Charming fellow is.
Dandini Nor I, My Lord, nor I.
King He'd be just the sort of fellow to marry my daughter, eh? What d'you think?
Dandini I don't think so, sire.
King Not good enough for her?

Dandini It's not that, Your Majesty.
King You're not trying to say that she's not good enough for him?
Dandini No, no, Your Highness: you don't have a daughter.
King Of course I don't, it was silly of you to suggest such a thing. Whose is that palace in the distance, eh?

Hopefully the audience will claim it for "The prince" but if not Dandini must say: "That Puss-in-Boots says it belongs to his master, the prince, but I thought it was an ogre who lived there"

King Interesting!

Puss emerges from hiding, apparently distraught

Puss Help! Help! Don't let them get away with them! Help! Stop thieves! Help! Help!
King My goodness, look Dandini, it's ... what's-his-name in boots.
Dandini Puss!
King Yes! I say — you there in the ... in the ...
Dandini Boots!
King Yes! What's the matter — Puss in Boots — what's afoot?
Puss *(on his knees to the King)* Oh, Your Majesty, did you see them, did you see them?
King I don't know, did I, Dandini? Did I see them?
Dandini Who?
Puss The thieves, the rascals that stole my master's clothes.
King Thieves? Robbers?
Puss My master, the prince ——
King Charming.
Puss — that's him — was out on his estates. He fancied a swim in a nearby pool, and while he was in the water some thieves stole all his rich clothes and jewellery ——
King You can't trust anyone these days.
Puss — so now my master has no clothes to wear.
King I'll bet they took my bunny rabbit, Dandini.
Dandini How embarrassing.
King I'm rabbit-less and the prince is clothes-less.
Puss That's it, Your Majesty.
King Where is he, this prince of yours?
Puss *(pointing)* Over there, Your Highness.
King *(looking off)* Oh yes, you're right, he has no clothes on ... *(Calling)* Yoo! hoo! Hallo prince!

Act II, Scene 2

Colin shrieks a little shriek, off

He's looking a little chilly too. (*To Dandini*) Quick Dandini, nip back to the castle and get some clothes for the prince, something suitable, quality, rich — something as befits a prince. (*Calling off*) We're getting you something, keep calm. (*To Dandini*) Off you go, Dandini.
Dandini My Lord. (*He makes to exit*)
King Oh, just a second, leave your cloak; the poor fellow can't stay in the water too long, he'll go all wrinkly ...
Dandini Yes, sire.

Dandini leaves his cloak with Puss and exits through the auditorium

Puss exits to the "pond" to rescue Colin, carrying the cloak

King Yes, I'll bet those robbers took my bunny rabbit. I certainly wouldn't put it past them. If you'd pinch clothes you certainly wouldn't draw the line at rabbits.

Puss and Colin enter, Colin wrapped in the cloak

Ha! There you are ... You look more like a prince than before ...
Colin Do I?
King Goodness me, yes. You didn't see them get my rabbit, did you?
Colin Rabbit?
King Thought not. Look, better not wait around here for Dandini to come back, you could catch a severe cold. Why not stroll up to the castle with me, have a spot of food, put the clothes on. I'll introduce you to my daughter.
Colin What? Oh yes, I'd like that. (*To Puss, sotto voce*) Did you hear that, Puss? A daughter.
Puss (*to Colin, sotto voce*) Yes, I heard, but I think you should know ——
Colin (*to Puss, sotto voce*) Fame and fortune.

The King, Puss and Colin move down an aisle towards an exit

King Yes she'll be pleased to meet you, I'm sure, Charming. Just keep your eyes open for a rabbit as we go; a little fella he is ...
Colin I will, Your Majesty, I will!
Puss A rabbit. I know where that came from ...

And from the rear of the stage comes the booming voice of the Ogre

Ogre (*off*) Keep away from my palace! Keep out of my forests! All these lands are mine!

King Who said that?
Colin My Lord?
King Sounded like an ogre to me. He lived in your palace before you did, you know. Come on.

The King exits

Ogre (*off*) Trespassers will not only be prosecuted — they will be eaten alive.
Colin Did you hear that, Puss?

Puss nods

I think you'd better go and explain that he's living in my palace.

Colin exits

Puss ventures towards the stage area

Ogre (*off*) And that means you too, Pussy-Cat.

Puss freezes, terrified

Black-out

CURTAIN

ACT III

Scene 1

The House Lights dim and in the semi-darkness we hear the booming voice of the Ogre (over a megaphone or an off-stage microphone)

Ogre (*off*) No trespassers! No visitors! No entrance! Keep away! Beware the Ogre! Message ends!

The Lights come up on Puss C in front of the Curtain. *He has a pouch, purse, bag or box with him*

Puss (*to the audience*) I'm not scared, I'm not frightened — I'm terrified! I've never dealt with an ogre before; I've never met, never ever seen one — but I don't like the sound of them, I know that. But I've got to do it. Fame and fortune I promised him, and a promise is a promise. I'll just take a little look. (*He peers through the* Curtain) There doesn't seem to be anyone about inside; perhaps he's on holiday. Let's go and have a look, eh? Shall we?

With or without the audience's agreement, Puss enters the Ogre's palace by going through the Curtain, *which rises as he passes through, revealing:*

The Ogre's kitchen. Everything we see is big

(*Quietly*) Hallo! Anybody there? Hallo! Mr Ogre? Are you there? Anybody? Hallo! I've come to read the meter! Is anybody home? (*To the audience*) There certainly doesn't seem to be anyone about; of course, he could have just nipped out to the shops, I suppose. I'll try shouting, shall I? Just in case he's asleep. But perhaps I don't want to wake him ... Oh, what'll I do?

Puss sits somewhere convenient. Just as he does so we hear the sound of heavy footsteps approaching. Puss is transfixed. The steps come closer and closer

Ogre (*off*) I know you're there.
Puss Oh! Oh!
Ogre (*off*) You can't hide from me.

Puss tries to hide, ending up half-hidden and suitably scared

(*Off*) I'll find you wherever you are.

The Ogre enters. He is a small ogre with a megaphone

Did you hear me?

Puss, still half-hidden, nods frantically. The Ogre moves warily round the room, on tip-toe, half-heartedly searching for the intruder. When he discovers Puss, they both jump

Ogre ⎫ (*together*) Aaah!
Puss ⎭
Ogre Don't do that!
Puss You frightened me.
Ogre Well, you scared me, hiding there.
Puss Keep your voice down. Come on, you can hide with me. Come on!
Ogre What d'you mean?
Puss Hide! Come on, don't argue, do it!

The Ogre hides with Puss. There's a pause

Ogre Could I just ——
Puss Sssh! Keep quiet! (*Pause*) I think he's perhaps gone. I'll look, you stay there ...
Ogre But I ——
Puss Sssh! Keep there; I'll just check for us ... (*He comes out of the hiding place and looks around the room*) It's all right, I think you can come out now — come on!

The Ogre emerges

That was a close one.
Ogre Was it?
Puss We might have been caught; we might still if he comes back. If he does we'll have to hide again.
Ogre If you say so.
Puss What are you doing here anyway?
Ogre I was going to ask you that.
Puss Did you sneak in here like me?
Ogre No, no, I live here.
Puss What? You actually live here?

Act III, Scene 1

Ogre Yep!
Puss So you're one of the Ogre's servants?
Ogre Nope!
Puss Oh!
Ogre I'm the Ogre.
Puss You're the Ogre?
Ogre Sure am! But you can call me Terry.
Puss Terry?
Ogre Short for Terrifying, Man-eating, Awesome Ogre, Plantagenet III.
Puss Terry the Ogre.
Ogre The full title's a bit long, I only use it on formal occasions and when I visit Cruft's.
Puss But — you're not like I imagined an Ogre would be.
Ogre Well I have my off days, you know. In fact I've been feeling rather peaky recently.
Puss I thought you'd be bigger somehow.
Ogre I've been poorly.
Puss You sounded bigger just now, and outside; it was a big voice.
Ogre Technology.
Puss And I thought you'd be ugly.
Ogre Ugly? Well ... Come back at full moon, things get rather ugly then — and Hallowe'en's quite good too; quite a get-together.
Puss You've got quite a reputation around the place for being big and ugly, and ——
Ogre And what? What?
Puss Well — anti-social. You know eating people and —that sort of thing.
Ogre Village gossip.
Puss Really?
Ogre Although I do have my moments.
Puss Tell me more.
Ogre Well, when you're an ogre, there's a lot expected of you, you've got a lot to live up to. People make assumptions. They know what they want of an ogre.
Puss I'm sure you're right.
Ogre Oh, I am, I am. Now I'll let you into a little secret: sometimes I am vicious, and big, really big, you know gigantic — but it's all an act.
Puss Some act.
Ogre And it's all because I can change my appearance as and when I want to. Big, small, vicious, calm, any shape, any form I like, just as the need arises.
Puss Sounds like quite a trick.
Ogre Oh it is! It is! Would you like me to show you? I could do the Man-eating Vicious Beast if you like?

Puss No! No! It's not necessary. I've just called, actually, to see if you'd like to move out, you know leave this palace and all the riches it contains, and go live somewhere else — let somebody else move in. What do you think?
Ogre I think I feel the Man-eating Beast coming on.
Puss It was just a thought; it was such a good cause.
Ogre That's what they all say.
Puss And it would give you a chance to see how the rest of the world lives; a bit of travel, you know, broaden your mind, extend your experiences.
Ogre I never looked at it that way ...
Puss But you were saying about being able to change your shape ... your form. I'll bet you can't really do it.
Ogre You mean the Man-eating Vicious Beast?
Puss Well, I thought perhaps something smaller ——
Ogre I do a good snake.
Puss — smaller ... What about — say — a mouse?
Ogre Mouse? A mouse? Easy, I can do a mouse any time.
Puss You can't!
Ogre Can so.
Puss Never.
Ogre I tell you I can.
Puss Prove it.
Ogre Close your eyes then.
Puss Oh, some trick; if you're so good at it, then do it, here — and — now!
Ogre I will! I will then! Mr clever Puss in Boots, just you watch — I'll be a mouse in no time.
Puss I'm waiting.

The Ogre stands at the rear of the stage and concentrates so hard that it hurts

I don't see any mouse ... Come on, if you're so clever, do it. (*He turns to the audience*) I don't think he can — I think he's been telling me ——

Bang! Flash! At the rear of stage, the Ogre exits and is replaced by a mouse

Wow! You did it! (*He pounces and catches the mouse.*) Got you! Now all I've got to do is to eat you up and the palace and all its contents belong to my master. Shall I eat you now?

The audience may not wish this

No ... I'll save you, because you're quite a nice ogre. I'll put you in here (*the pouch, purse, bag or box*) — you can't make yourself bigger in there. And now I can go and tell my master that everything is his: fame and fortune, courtesy of Puss in Boots. (*He bows and gives a flourish*)

Act III, Scene 2   45

The Lights on the kitchen fade and the CURTAIN *falls*

SCENE 2

Outside the two houses

Martha and Cinderella emerge from Cinderella's door. Martha carries a long, long list of wishes

Cinderella — and some of that really expensive perfume, and skis, and tickets for the opera, and a yacht, and a tennis court, and a castle of my own, and ... did I mention a holiday?
Martha Several times.
Cinderella Because it's most important.
Martha More important than going to the King's birthday ball?
Cinderella Oh no! That's the mostest importantest wish of them all.
Martha Then that's the one we'll start with, eh?
Cinderella Yes, let's.
Martha Now, there are various things that I will need for the magic spell.
Cinderella Things that you need?
Martha Well, now, you can't make an omelette without eggs, can you? And you can't make spells without ingredients.
Cinderella Like cooking?
Martha Bally bundles, you've got it. So, here's what I'll need: a pumpkin!
Cinderella A pumpkin.
Martha Six mice, a rat and two lizards.
Cinderella Funny sort of recipe.
Martha They've all got their parts to play, so off you go and find them.
Cinderella I don't have to, I can wish for them — put them on my list.
Martha Ah, well now, that's an interesting idea but it won't work. I need the things to change into the new things; if I wanted to wish a pumpkin I'd have to start with a glass coach, you see, but since we want a glass coach, we have to start with a pumpkin.
Cinderella Oh, I see!
Martha So you just nip off my dear into the back garden and get the things we need, and the sooner the better; after all you don't want to be late for the ball, do you?
Cinderella I'm on my way, I'll be back in no time.

Cinderella makes to leave

Drusilla and Blusilla enter from their house

Drusilla Ah, there you are, Cinderella.

Blusilla We've been looking for you.
Drusilla We need you to sort out some of the clothes that belonged to Father.
Blusilla It's for our gentleman visitor.
Drusilla Something good, mind you.
Blusilla Elegant.
Drusilla Well, posh really.
Blusilla Because he's escorting me to the King's ball.
Drusilla No, he's escorting me, Bloo.
Blusilla That's not what he said, Droo.
Drusilla But he can't talk, he's lost his voice; how could he say anything?
Blusilla He mimed.
Drusilla Well, I never heard him.
Blusilla So go on, Cinderella, do it! Now! Shoo!

Cinderella exits as she says the following line

Cinderella I've just got to go down the garden first.
Drusilla Oh, she always leaves it 'til the last minute.
Martha She's getting a pumpkin.
Blusilla Oh, I wouldn't say that; she's filling out a bit, but she's a growing girl, what d'you expect?
Drusilla And her mother always was a bit on the large side.
Blusilla Come on, Droo, we'll have to go and get ourselves ready.
Drusilla Coming, Bloo; then we'll have to dress our gentleman visitor in his new clothes.
Blusilla I'm looking forward to that.
Drusilla So am I!
Blusilla I'm all — you know — at the thought.
Drusilla So am I!
Blusilla }
Drusilla } *(together)* Let's do it — now! Come on.

They head for the exit, ad-libbing to Cinderella "Have you got the clothes?" etc., as they go

Drusilla I'll do his vest!
Blusilla I'll do his ... pants!
Drusilla Ooh, no I want to do those: I'll swap you.
Blusilla We could do a leg each.
Drusilla We could work in unison.
Blusilla Let's go and warm our hands.

They exit

Act III, Scene 2   47

Martha (*to the audience*) Poor fella, fancy being in their hands. Sure it'll be like being dressed by a couple of chimpanzees — and he won't be able to say a word about it!

Cinderella emerges with a pumpkin and a bag and some of Colin's clothes

Cinderella One pumpkin, five mice, two lizards, but no rat; however, I've put a few snails in instead.
Martha No rat? Then there's no coachman, and only five horses if there's only five mice, but if there's no coachman to drive them then you'll never get there ... Now what can we do about that?
Cinderella But look what else I found, just thrown away into our garden ... (*She shows Martha the clothes*)
Martha They're just old rags, ignore them.
Cinderella No, you don't understand. I recognize them; they're Colin's from next door. What d'you think's happened to him?
Martha I've no idea ... now where can I be finding a rat?
Cinderella Perhaps he's been eaten by the Ogre, or perhaps he's drowned — what do you think? Oh dear!
Martha Don't worry, Cinderella, think about the ball.
Cinderella But I quite liked him, we'd a lot in common: we're both poor and put-upon ... and ... (*she produces the whistle from Colin's clothes*) oh look, here's a whistle in his pocket.
Martha (*apprehensively*) A whistle!
Cinderella I'll give it a blow. (*She blows the whistle*)
Martha I've a feeling I know what'll happen next.
Cinderella I didn't hear anything — did you?
Martha No, I didn't, but I think I know a cat who did.
Cinderella What?
Martha Let's get these things inside — for the spell — and we need to do the ballgown as well ...
Cinderella Why didn't it whistle? (*She blows the whistle again*)

Puss enters down the aisle, through the auditorium

Puss Stop! Don't do it any more! My ears won't stand it —stop! Stop! Stop! And where did you get that whistle anyway?
Martha Bally blankets I was right!
Cinderella Who are you?
Puss (*with a bow and a flourish*) Puss in Boots at your service, ma'am.
Martha Just what we're needing at the minute.
Puss I am?
Cinderella He is?
Martha Well, it should really be a rat, but I reckon you're pretty close.

Puss A rat? Me?
Martha We're just needing your help for tonight.
Puss Tonight? Oh, I can't help tonight, I'm going to the ball.
Martha That's right, you will be! Just step inside.

Martha goes into the house

Cinderella You don't happen to have a spare mouse on you do you?
Puss A mouse?
Cinderella That you could lend me, just for tonight ... I'm one short.
Puss It's your lucky night ... (*He holds up the box or bag with the mouse in it*))
Cinderella That's great! Now we've got all we need. Come inside.

Cinderella and Puss go into Cinderella's house

There could be some "magic" music here, and a lighting change and an explosion off and lots of exclamations of admiration

SCENE 3

The CURTAIN *rises. We are in an ante-room in the King's palace, decorated for a birthday. Music plays in the background*

The King and Dandini are on stage

King I am, I am — I'm all excited! I've even got over losing the ... what's-his-name ... Oh, why can't we have a birthday every year?
Dandini You can, Your Highness.
King Then I will, I most certainly will. That must be one of the best ideas I've ever had, Dandini, don't you think?
Dandini I don't know how you do it, My Lord, I really don't.
King I must tell the queen about it immediately.
Dandini No, sire.
King Won't she want to know?
Dandini You aren't married, Your Highness.
King Quite right. I was just testing you, that's all.

Colin enters, resplendent in new finery

Colin (*with a bow*) Your Majesty!
King Eh? Oh, yes, yes, hallo, Prince ...
Dandini (*sotto voce*) Charming.

Act III, Scene 3

King I remember, I remember.
Dandini (*sotto voce*) We lent him the clothes, My Lord.
King I know, I know — I recall ...
Dandini (*sotto voce*) He sent you a gift of a rabbit.
King I remember everything, Lord Dandini, everything; (*to Colin*) and how are you, my boy?
Colin Very well indeed, sire.
King Your mother can't be here tonight, nor can your sister, the princess, but it's good to have you home, my son.
Dandini What!
Colin You're too kind, My Lord, Your Majesty.
King Just call me "Dad".
Dandini But Your Highness ——
King Something wrong, Dandini?
Dandini (*anything for a quiet life*) No, no, nothing, sire. I was just thinking that it'll be easier for you — for us all — now that you've actually got a son ...
King Of course it will; the best birthday present a King can have.
Dandini Charming.
Colin That's me.

There is a tableau of the three of them

> *Martha enters with Drusilla, Blusilla and Caleb; they hover behind her. Martha is now acting as a sort of major-domo*

Martha Your Majesty, my lords, ladies and gentlemen, the sisters Drusilla and Blusilla Pinchpenny and their escort ... er ... (*she has no name for him*) their escort ——

Drusilla whispers to Martha

— their escort the big man from next door.
King Welcome! Welcome! So you are?
Drusilla Drusilla, Your Majesty. (*She curtsies*)
King (*to Blusilla*) Then you must be the big man from next door.
Blusilla Ooh, you are silly!

Blusilla pushes the King

> No! This is him ... here ... *look.*

She drags Caleb forward

> See.

King (*recovering his breath*) Oh yes! Welcome. You are most welcome.
Drusilla You have to forgive his not speaking, Your Highness.
Blusilla He swallowed something that disagreed with him. (*To Caleb*) Bow to the king.

Caleb bows

King I hope it will not stop his enjoyment of the proceedings. Can I introduce my Chancellor, Lord Dandini.
Drusilla Ooh, Bloo — he'll do!
Blusilla Ooh, Droo — me too!
Dandini (*with a bow*) Ladies!
Blusilla Ooh, Droo, isn't he something else.
Drusilla Than what dear?

Blusilla explains what she meant to Drusilla during the following line

King (*introducing Colin*) And this is my son, the Prince Charming.
Blusilla Ooh!
Drusilla Ooh!

The effect of Prince Charming's appearance on Caleb is even stronger than it was on the sisters. Caleb reacts melodramatically. He goes to Colin and grabs him, looking closer: is it, isn't it? He examines Colin's clothes. He tries to speak, mouthing words.

King We can't hear a word he says.
Drusilla His voice has gone.
King He seems to think he knows you.
Colin I've never seen him before in my life.

Caleb makes to punch Colin, but he is held back by Drusilla and Blusilla

Drusilla Don't do that, dear — we're guests.
Blusilla You don't punch princes of the realm.
Drusilla It's treason.
Blusilla Treason for what dear?
Drusilla No dear, you don't understand ... (*To Caleb*) You can explain when your voice comes back.
King Shall we join the others?

Everyone on stage freezes in a pose

Act III, Scene 3   51

Martha But before anybody could go anywhere, wasn't it herself who made her entrance? The others were spellbound — quite apt really.

Cinderella enters to a central position

(*Announcing*) The Princess Priscilla! (*To the audience*) Well she looks like one — so she should sound like one. The company was amazed ——

They all look amazed

— and quite took aback.

All on stage take a pace away from Cinderella

Martha And Drusilla said:
Drusilla Tut! Just look at that Bloo!
Martha And Blusilla said:
Blusilla Tut! Overdressed by far, Droo!
Martha And Caleb said ... oh, he didn't say anything, of course — 'cos he couldn't, poor fella! So the prince said:
Colin Wow! Wow!
Martha Not inspired, I know, but enthusiastic, and the King said ...
King She looks beautiful; she could be my daughter.
Martha Wishful thinking indeed, but Dandini said:
Dandini Who knows, sire, she might yet be .
Martha Which was quite clever of him under the circumstances, don't you think? Then the prince spoke again:
Colin Haven't we met somewhere before?

The atmosphere is broken by all the rest of the cast saying "Aw!", meaning "What a trite question."

Cinderella Well — you do look a little familiar, too.
Colin Do you come here often?

Another "Aw!" from those on stage

Martha (*to the audience*) He's not doing too well is he? ... Perhaps they'd better dance. Your Majesty, my lords, ladies and gentlemen, the dancing has commenced.
King Dancing! Oh good! Dancing! I like that, don't I, Dandini? Come on, everyone, come on, this way ...

And everyone except Martha ad-libs off

Martha They'll be able to talk while they're dancing, and they haven't got long, you know, these spells of mine don't last for ever ... In fact, young Cinderella there has got to be home by ... Oh now what time was it? D'you know I'd forget me own head if it were loose. She's got to be home by ...

Hopefully the audience will help; if not, Martha will have to remember the time herself. However, let's assume she's prompted

Midnight! Yes, that's right. Fancy your knowing that. Are you a Fairy Godmother too? No? Well you've got the knowledge so perhaps the skill will come in time.

The clock strikes midnight

My goodness me, Bally busfares, isn't that the midnight hour this very minute? Isn't it amazing how time flies when you're having fun. Now where the devil is the girl? The spell will disappear before you can say — — (*she calls off*) Cinderella! Priscilla! Come on!

Cinderella runs across the stage and off the other side

Martha Come on, my dear, there's no time to waste.

Colin runs on, clutching a slipper

Colin Wait! Stop! Come back — I wanted to talk more. Priscilla! Come back — oh, heck!
Martha Never mind, Prince Charming.
Colin What?
Martha I said never mind. Look what you have in your hand.
Colin Pardon? Oh, yes, it's her slipper, she dropped it — well, it fell off her foot as she ran out.
Martha I said she was a three, but she would insist on a four.
Colin Four what?
Martha Don't worry your prince's little head; just think, all you have to do is find the girl whose foot this slipper fits and you can reclaim your princess.
Colin No, I don't! Don't be stupid.

Martha is gobsmacked

I know who she is, don't I? It's Cinderella — I used to live next door to her. I know where she lives; I can nip round any time.

Act III, Scene 4

Martha Wait! Hold it there; now just you be after realizing one or two things, me boy-o! You can't let on you already know her without explaining how, and if you do, then the whole story comes out, and in no time at all you won't be Prince Charming any more. No fame, and certainly no fortune. Think about that.

Drusilla, Blusilla, Caleb, the King and Dandini enter; ad-lib "Where is she?", "Why did she run off?", "Where's the Princess gone?", "Who was she?", "Did you catch her?", "Did you see which way she went?", etc.

Colin Too late.

They all quieten

She has gone! Who knows where? And yet, wait — she left her slipper behind in her haste. All I have to do is to go around the kingdom until I find the girl whose foot this slipper fits ... and then I will have rediscovered my own princess.
Martha (*to the audience*) ... That's my boy!

The onstage crowd discuss the situation together, ad lib

The CURTAIN *falls, leaving Martha in front of it*

SCENE 4

Outside the two houses

Martha (*to the audience*) Sometimes you've just got to keep the story on the straight and narrow. Well, of course he started out with the slipper the very next day. He didn't go straight to Cinderella's 'cos that would have been a bit too obvious ...

Puss enters from Cinderella's house

Puss I'm not doing that any more! That's the last time I do anyone a favour. I'm worn out, I was up all night.
Martha I thought you were a good rat — you did very well.
Puss Driving coaches is not my idea of fun.

The Ogre enters from Cinderella's house, now back to his small human form

Ogre Wow! Hey, wasn't that great? Wasn't that just the greatest? Galloping through the forest, over hill, over dale, bridges — whoosh! — gone in a flash, the clattering of hooves, the thrill of the chase, all the way there and then gallop, gallop, home again, home again. What a night!
Puss Shut up!
Ogre The cool evening air in your nostrils, the whole team working together. On! On we raced.
Puss You nearly pulled my arms out.
Ogre I enjoyed every minute of it.
Martha (*indicating the Ogre*) And who's this little spalpeen then?
Puss Oh ... this — this is Terry.
Martha Top of the milk to you.
Ogre Pleased to meet you.
Martha I'm a fairy godmother.
Ogre I'm an ogre.
Puss Don't be modest.
Ogre Sorry — I'm the Ogre.
Martha Well, you don't look much like the Ogre to me.
Puss Don't tempt him.
Ogre I've never had so much fun for a long time ... It's better than ogre-ing, being normal can be quite fun — can't it?
Martha }
Puss } (*together*) Are you asking us?
Ogre I think I'll try it for a while.

The King, Dandini and Colin enter with the slipper on a cushion down the auditorium aisle

Martha (*resuming her major-domo role*) Pray silence and make way for His Majesty the King.
King ... and I've noticed she's not been at breakfast for months — it could be even longer. I said to the toastmaster this morning, I said "Won't the queen be with us?" and he said ——
Dandini (*looking round*) Haven't we been here before?
King That's right, Lord Dandini; and how many more girls have we to see today?
Dandini Quite a few, Your Majesty, quite a few.
King And who do we see here?
Martha The sisters Drusilla and Blusilla Pinchpenny.
Colin No chance.
Martha (*to Colin*) Sssh! Don't give the game away.
King Come out, come out wherever you are!

Drusilla and Blusilla emerge

Act III, Scene 4   55

Drusilla Oh Bloo, look it's our turn with the slipper.
Blusilla I'm eager, Droo, I'm eager.
Drusilla I'm eager too, Bloo, like you.
Blusilla Ooh! Coo, Droo, listen, if it's me, not you, which I'm sure it will be, then you can be my bridesmaid.
Drusilla And if it's me, not you, like it will be, then you won't even be invited ...
Blusilla Ooh, boo-hoo, Droo!
Drusilla Ooh, don't be a silly — sausage, I don't mean it.
King And who is who?
Drusilla I'm Droo.
Blusilla And I'm Bloo.
King (*to Drusilla*) Let the slipper be tried — on you.

Dandini tries the slipper on Drusilla

Colin (*to Martha*) Where's Cinderella?
Martha She must still be inside.
Colin She should be here too.
Drusilla It fits! It fits!
Dandini No, it doesn't.
Drusilla Screw it on a bit harder — then it will.

Dandini bangs the slipper hard on to Drusilla's foot

   Not like that, you'll cripple me. Have you got one in a wider fitting?
King Next, please.
Blusilla It's me, not you, Droo, ooh — this is it.

Dandini tries the slipper on Blusilla

Colin (*to Martha*) She should be here! Why isn't she?

Martha shrugs

Blusilla It fits! It fits!
Dandini No, it doesn't.
Blusilla Perhaps you've got the wrong foot — try the other one.

Dandini tries the slipper on Blusilla's other foot

   Ow! Don't do that, it hurts. Have you something in pink suede, with a sling back?

King Next, please.
Drusilla There is no-one.
Blusilla No-one at all.
Ogre I'll have a try if you like ... (*He sits down to try the slipper on*)
Puss No, don't. Give up while you're winning.
Colin Wait! There is someone else. Where is Cinderella?

Drusilla and Blusilla gasp

Drusilla How did you know about her?
Blusilla She's a mere nothing — she doesn't count.
Drusilla Have you been peeping through keyholes?
King Is there someone else then?
Colin My Lord, I believe they have a stepsister.
King You know so much. Let her be brought.
Drusilla Oh, very well!
Blusilla Oh stinky-poo, Droo!
Drusilla (*shouting off*) Bring her out!

Caleb emerges holding Cinderella; he's obviously been restraining her

Cinderella Let me go you great oaf! Keep your hands off me!
King Let the rabbit be tried on!
Dandini The slipper, My Lord.
King Oh yes, the — er — slipper.

Dandini tries the slipper on Cinderella; it fits. There are gasps of wonderment from everyone. They all freeze

Martha And of course the slipper fitted perfectly — as I bet you all guessed, and everyone went back to the castle to celebrate.

They all ad-lib "congratulations"

Scene 5

The Curtain *rises and we're back at the castle. The cast adopt a tableau*

Martha It's living-happily-ever-after time. Cinderella — or should we call her Princess Priscilla — and Prince Charming lived — happily ever after. Then there were Drusilla and Caleb and Blusilla and Lord Dandini —

Act III, Scene 5

there's a couple of unlikely couples! The ogre was so happy being normal he gave Prince Charming his palace as a wedding present. So Puss in Boots had gained his master the fame and fortune he'd promised him. As for the King ——

The tableau breaks

King (*to Martha*) Ah, there you are, my dear. I have missed you around the place, especially at breakfast. What a good time to come home; our son is just about to get married.
Martha Our son!
King Prince Charming: you remember him?
Martha (*to the audience*) I do — but does he?
King Come and congratulate them, my Queen.
Martha (*to the audience*) Queen? Ah, well; if you can't beat 'em ... join 'em.

Martha joins the others

King Toast! A toast all round! That's what we need! A toast!

Puss and the Ogre exit and return bringing drinks

This isn't toast! Never mind, let's drink to everyone's health, happiness and rabbits.

They all drink a toast, ad-libbing "Health", "Happiness", and "Rabbits". Caleb chokes on his drink

Drusilla Are you all right, my dear?
Caleb (*nodding, coughing, then, to Puss*) You! It's you! At last! You're the cause of all this, you, Puss in Boots. *Give me my boots now!*

A wild chase ensues on which the play ends, as all the cast chase about the auditorium and finally exit

CURTAIN

FURNITURE AND PROPERTY LIST

ACT I

Scene 1

On stage: Pile of old clothes, rags, rubbish

Scene 2

On stage: Two sets of kitchen furniture
COLIN'S KITCHEN:
Boots
Polishing cloth
Scarf
CINDERELLA'S KITCHEN:
Shawl

Off stage: Small bell (**Martha**)
Bag containing Christmas cards in envelopes, letter in envelope, three invitations in envelope, slip or pad, pen, small parcel containing whistle (**Martha**)
Two cards (**Puss**)
Garments (**Cinderella**)

Personal: **Puss**: bag containing diary

ACT II

Scene 1

On stage: Ante-room furniture

Off stage: Table-cloth (**Drusilla** and **Blusilla**)
Small pile of objects including Colin's whistle (**Caleb**)

Scene 2

On stage: Forest setting

Furniture and Property List

ACT III

Scene 1

On stage: **Ogre**'s kitchen setting with giant kitchen furniture and properties

Off stage: Megaphone (**Ogre**)

Scene 2

On stage: Nil

Off stage: Long list of wishes (**Martha**)
Pumpkin, bag containing five mice, two lizards, a few snails, **Colin**'s clothes and whistle (**Cinderella**)
Slipper on cushion (**King, Dandini, Colin**)

Scene 3

On stage: Ante-room setting and furniture; decorated for a birthday

Scene 4

On stage: Nil

Off stage: Slipper on cushion (**King, Dandini, Colin**)
Drinks (**Puss** and **Ogre**)

Scene 5

On stage: Ante-room setting

Off stage: Drinks (**Puss** and **Ogre**)

LIGHTING PLOT

Practical fittings required: nil
Various interior and exterior settings

ACT I, SCENE 1

To open: Pre-set on heap of clothes, etc.

No cues

ACT I, SCENE 2

To open: Lighting on kitchen settings and forestage

No cues

ACT II, SCENE 1

To open: General lighting on ante-room and forestage

Cue 1   The CURTAIN falls on ante-room setting   (Page 31)
           Cut lights on ante-room setting

ACT II, SCENE 2

To open: Lighting on forestage

Cue 2   **Puss** freezes, terrified   (Page 40)
        Black-out

ACT III, SCENE 1

To open: Semi-darkness

Cue 3   **Puss** goes through the CURTAIN   (Page 41)
          Bring up lights on **Ogre'**s *kitchen and forestage*

Lighting Plot

Cue 4	**Puss**: "Puss in Boots." Bow and flourish *Fade lights on* **Ogre**'s *kitchen*	(Page 45)

ACT III, SCENE 2

To open: Lighting on forestage and two doors

Cue 5	Magic music *Lighting change*	(Page 48)

ACT III, SCENE 3

To open: Lighting on ante-room setting

No cues

ACT III, SCENE 4

To open: Lighting on forestage and two doors

No cues

ACT III, SCENE 5

To open: Lighting on ante-room setting

No cues

EFFECTS PLOT

ACT I

Cue 1   **Martha**: "Oh, bally bunions!"   (Page 23)
            Flash

ACT II

Cue 2   C<small>URTAIN</small> 1 rises   (Page 24)
            Flash

Cue 3   **Cinderella**: " ... had one right now."   (Page 34)
            Bang and flash

ACT III

Cue 4   **Puss**: " I think he's been telling me ——"   (Page 44)
            Bang and flash

Cue 5   **Cinderella** and **Puss** go into the house   (Page 48)
            Magic music, segueing into party music;
            fade when appropriate

Cue 6   **Martha**: " ... perhaps the skill will come in time."   (Page 52)
            Clock strikes midnight

A licence issued by Samuel French Ltd to perform this play does not include permission to use the Incidental music specified in this copy. Where the place of performance is already licensed by the P<small>ERFORMING</small> R<small>IGHT</small> S<small>OCIETY</small> a return of the music used must be made to them. If the place of performance is not so licensed then application should be made to the Performing Right Society, 29 Berners Street, London W1.

A separate and additional licence from P<small>HONOGRAPHIC</small> P<small>ERFORMANCES</small> L<small>TD</small>, Ganton House, Ganton Street, London W1 is needed whenever commercial recordings are used.

www.ingramcontent.com/pod-product-compliance
Ingram Content Group UK Ltd.
Pitfield, Milton Keynes, MK11 3LW, UK
UKHW021847210426
5322IPUK00022B/511